50 QUEER MUSIC ICONS

WHO CHANGED THE WORLD

A CELEBRATION OF LGBTQ+ LEGENDS

50 QUEER MUSIC ICONS

WHO CHANGED THE WORLD

A CELEBRATION OF LGBTQ+ LEGENDS

WILL LARNACH-JONES
ILLUSTRATED BY MICHELE ROSENTHAL

hardie grant books

CONTENTS

INTRODUCTION

Since time immemorial, music has captured the hearts and minds of the world. In the last half century, pop music has been co-joined with pop culture, each decade's changing fashions, trends and cultural values reflected in the hits blasting over TV, radio and the world wide web.

Throughout the years, music has been the conduit through which many queer artists have chosen to express themselves, some screaming from the rooftops out-and-proud, others lurking in the shadows, or even hiding in plain sight.

As beautiful and varied as the LGBTQ+ community itself, queer musicians have been pivotal players in creating new genres, breaking down musical and social boundaries, and always running ahead of the curve. One way or another, the queer music icons amongst these pages all changed the dial, some harmoniously marrying their art and sexuality, others allowing their music to speak for itself, others struggling to live authentically in the public gaze. Other icons featured are not exclusively LGBTQ+, but have become part of the queer story through a combination of their creative output, life story or open-minded advocacy.

From protest singers and disco divas to genderfucking hip hop experimentalists, these musical pioneers inspire, infuriate and entertain in equal measures. This book serves as an introduction to our rich queer musical heritage. Further listening greatly encouraged.

WITH THE ARRIVAL OF THE NOUGHTIES, GOLDFRAPP HERALDED A NEW ERA OF INTELLIGENT POP: FARE THEE WELL BANDS SUCH AS STEPS.

Singer Alison Goldfrapp (b. 13 May 1966) was something to behold. An explosion of cherubic curls and sullen pout, she presented as a short-fused indie diva with extraordinary vocal range and low tolerance for bullshit. Both onstage and off, Goldfrapp was in control of her career, image and sexuality, whichever way she chose to direct her gaze.

An ex-convent school tearaway, Goldfrapp spent her youth faffing about Bristol's music and art scenes. Her music came into focus after meeting creative partner in crime Will Gregory, who had chanced upon her guest vocal on Tricky's 'Pumpkin' (1995). His music-as-soundscape approach proved the perfect foil for Goldfrapp's experimental vocal approach. From operatic soprano to ugly wails, it was as though her off-kilter lyrics and melodies drew from the joy of words, forming and playing around in the mouth.

Debut longplayer *Felt Mountain* (2000) was a fascinating affair, its treated vocals and luscious strings forming pastoral idylls out of murky corners. While *Felt Mountain* was a slow burner, follow up *Black Cherry* (2003) was a slam dunk, kicking off a decade-long purple streak of bona fide pop hits.

A musical chameleon, Goldfrapp moved with silky ease between Weimar waltz to glitter stomp, Neu-disco to pagan pastoral. A fashion magpie to boot, Goldfrapp switched image with each album campaign: a black glitter Biba-esque fantasy, an air hostess for an imaginary fascist airline, a doe-eyed Pierrot carnival traveller.

Silver Eye (2017), the band's most recent album, saw Goldfrapp draw deeper into her creativity, photographing the album's art herself, a post-gender utopian future set against dramatic volcanic dunes and cobalt skies.

Announcing her same sex relationship in her mid forties did nothing to stymy her appeal, if anything quite the opposite. 'My sexuality is the same as my music and my life,' she quipped. 'Why does it need a label?'

ALISON GOLDFRAPP

CULTURE CLUB'S APPEARANCE ON *TOP OF THE POPS* WITH 'DO YOU REALLY WANT TO HURT ME' (1982) STIRRED A WOW AND FLUTTER NOT SEEN SINCE BOWIE'S 'STARMAN' PERFORMANCE A DECADE EARLIER. THE NEXT DAY, PLAYGROUNDS AND WORKSITES WERE ABLAZE WITH CONSTERNATION: WHO WAS THEIR EXTRAORDINARY SINGER?

Boy George (b. George Alan O'Dowd; 14 June 1961) had been working towards this moment all his life. From the doldrums of London's deepest suburbia, George's fanboy days following Bowie had propelled him on a musical path, leading to the punk and the New Romantic scenes.

As Blitz Club 'ace face' George wanted to to be 'someone'. Around him, other club regulars were having moments in the sun, either as one-hit wonders (Visage) or stadium fillers (Spandau Ballet).

A creative dalliance with Sex Pistols' manager Malcolm McLaren and punk upstarts Bow Wow Wow short circuited as soon as it began. George's own Culture Club eventually inked a deal, but it was the last-minute *Top of the Pops* slot that shot George into the public domain. To his fans – with his uber-ribboned hair and kabuki-like make-up – George was as safe as a plushy toy. A slew of pastel-hued hits, like 'Church of The Poisoned Mind' (1983) and 'Karma Chameleon' (1983), amassed, but as Culture Club collected Brits, Grammys and millions of sales, George was imploding. He soon crashed and burned – hounded and vilified in the UK's tabloid press for his heroin addiction.

He re-emerged, topping the charts with his first solo outing, the reggae-light of 'Everything I Own' (1987). Relieved from the confines of Culture Club, George was now an unapologetic right-on sister, 100% queer and outspoken. The Acid House explosion of the late 80s agreed with him, informing his gay protest track 'No Clause 28' (1988) and his second career as in-demand DJ. George has since had his ups and downs with the law and tabloids, outwitting and in many instances, outliving many of his contemporaries. Thirty years on, we're still mad about the boy.

BOY GEORGE

GERTRUDE 'MA RAINEY' PRIDGETT (B. 26 APRIL 1886 – D. 22 DEC. 1939) IS WIDELY HAILED AS THE 'MOTHER OF THE BLUES'. BORN TO A POOR FAMILY NOT LONG AFTER THE EMANCIPATION PROCLAMATION, HER GREGARIOUS PERSONA, POWERFUL VOICE AND ABILITY TO 'TELL IT LIKE IT IS' SAW HER HAILED AS THE FIRST EVER PROFESSIONAL BLUES SINGERS.

Performing from her early teens, Rainey was the 'Ma' in a double bill with her with her husband, the comic songster, Will, touring a circuit of tent shows and cabarets in the deep south. Rainey came into contact with the country blues, tales of day-to-day strife and struggle, which she worked into her own repertoire.

The hard work, heartbreak and woes of the blues held a mirror of everyday life to Rainey's audience. Her lyrics for songs such as 'Bo-Weevil Blues' (1923) and 'Prove It On Me Blues' (1928), also directly referenced her sexuality, from calling out men and their lack of sexual prowess to lesbian relationships and cross-dressing, concepts that were completely taboo in 'acceptable' society at the time.

Rainey was a larger than life presence on stage, donning wild horsehair wigs, long gowns and scatterings of diamonds. Under the spotlight, her gold teeth would sparkle, entrancing her audience, who hung on her every phrase, moaning and rocking as they 'felt' the blues with her.

Many credit Rainey as the early mentor (and rumoured sexual partner) of the mighty Bessie Smith, who in Rainey's wake would go onto even greater success as the 'Empress of the Blues'.

After the deaths of her mother and sister, Rainey retired from life on the road and returned to her hometown of Columbus, where she died just a few years later. Rainey was instrumental in spreading the blues from the ground up, in turn giving rise to jazz and rhythm and blues and laying down the foundations on which rock 'n' roll would be built.

MA RAINEY

LISA COLEMAN (B. 17 AUG. 1960) WAS THE RIPE OLD AGE OF 19 WHEN HIS ROYAL PURPLENESS, PRINCE, PLUCKED HER FROM OBSCURITY TO PLAY KEYS ON HIS 1980 ALBUM *DIRTY MIND*. THREE YEARS LATER, HER GIRLFRIEND WENDY MELVOIN (B. 26 JANUARY 1964) WOULD JOIN PRINCE'S MERRY TROUBADOURS, THE REVOLUTION. SO ENSUED A BONKERS THREE YEARS OF SMASH ALBUMS, FEATURE FILMS AND GLOBAL TOURING.

Wendy & Lisa had both been raised in households where music was the first language. Coleman's father was a respected session musician, and Melvoin's was a jazz pianist. Their families had been socially and creatively intertwined for as long as they could remember, even jamming and recording together. As teenagers, the girls' friendship transgressed to love, becoming a romantic couple for more than 20 years.

With The Revolution and his album and film *Purple Rain* (1984), Prince's career was at its creative and commercial zenith. Like an 80s Sly and the Family Stone, The Revolution straddled a racial and sexual spectrum, bringing together not just the best musicians but individuals who reflected Prince's prismed personality.

In 1986, the cherry popped and Prince cleared his creative slate, unceremoniously disbanding The Revolution. Wendy & Lisa struck it out as a duo, shooting out three quick fire albums by 1990. From the flickery, funky dream of 'Honeymoon Express' (1987), to the nu-jacky 'Satisfaction' (1989) and the drunk pendulum swing of 'Don't Try To Tell Me' (1990), these great songs were largely overlooked by the public.

Wendy & Lisa felt stymied by an industry who wanted to pigeonhole them as Lilith Fair 'granola' lesbians and to emulate their Prince-era success. Both options intruded their privacy and underminded the currency of their own creative merits. Undeterred, they've since lent their formidable chops to the likes of Seal, Neil Finn and Grace Jones. Film and TV opened a new world of work, winning awards and accolades for them and score work, including *Nurse Jackie* (2009) and *Heroes* (2009).

WENDY & LISA

FROM A DISTANCE (SEE WHAT I DID THERE?) POST WW2 HONOLULU SEEMED QUITE A REACH FROM THE RAZZLE DAZZLE OF BROADWAY. BETTE MIDLER (B. 1 DEC. 1945), HOWEVER, HAD STARS IN HER EYES, FASCINATED BY THE SEAMIER SIDE OF TOWN, THE RED LIGHT DISTRICT AND ITS MULTI-CULTI MIX OF SAILORS, SHOWGIRLS AND SPARKLE.

From childhood Midler was sass-tastic, a charismatic chatterbox with a gift for comedy and a passion to perform. The stage not only appealed as a way of life for Midler, but 'it was the only thing occurred to me, the only way out' of Hawaii. Majoring in drama, a bit part in the film *Hawaii* (1966) bought her a one-way ticket off the island.

Relocating to New York, Midler threw herself into a slew of off-Broadway productions, graduating to a three-year stint as Tzeitel in *Fiddler on The Roof*. Midler thrived in the theatre community, finding a sense of belonging that had eluded her at home.

Her broadway prowess lead to a residency at The Continental Baths, a gay bathhouse in the basement of The Ansonia Hotel. Re-christened as the Divine Miss M, Midler would draw upon her comedic chops and her love of old-time stars to play not only to the bathhouse boys, but every New York celeb you could flick a towel at.

Her residency lead to national TV appearances and a record deal, with her debut album, *The Divine Miss M* (1972), a Grammy-winning smash. 'Bathhouse Betty' had made it big.

As the 70s progressed Midler toured, recorded and turned to film, earning an Oscar nomination for her Joplin-inspired tragic heroine in *The Rose* (1979). Other 80s films saw her lend a campy touch to big mainstream comedies, before the tear-jerker *Beaches* (1989) destroyed us all with its knife to the heart, tragic storyline and plush powerballed 'Wind Beneath My Wings' (1988), a worldwide mega-hit.

A perennial favourite, fabulous and fiesty into her seventies, Midler remains umbilically connected to the gay audience who have been with her since day one.

BETTE MIDLER

★★ QUEER ICON ★★

Love of country chanteuse Patsy Cline inspired lang to form a tribute band, The Reclines; she was at the helm, sporting a spiky bonce and cowgirl outfits made from her mother's curtains.

While The Reclines was fun and games, this handsome prairie flower possessed a voice as smooth as a pebble lake and a bucketful of ambition. After a couple of albums Stateside, lang's duet of 'Crying' (1989) with Roy Orbison scored them both a Grammy.

Seymour Stein, he who discovered 'her Madgesty' Madonna, signed lang to Sire. Her country roots were ironed out for *Ingénue* (1992), a smoky foray into languid Adult Contemporary territory. With 'Constant Craving' constantly (ahem) on the radio, she scored a bona fide hit single and album, and a second Grammy.

Entering celebrity status lang graced the cover of *Vanity Fair*, soaped up in the barber's chair, on the receiving end of a razor shave from supermodel du jour Cindy Crawford.

lang also turned to acting, including queer classic *Salmonberries* (1991), and *Ellen's* now infamous coming-out episode (1997). Her fame was a soapbox to champion LGBTQ+ rights and animal welfare.

lang's duet album with legendary crooner Tony Bennett *A Wonderful World* (2002) scored her another Grammy. After a quieter spell, lang re-emerged in 2016, joining forces with Neko Case and Laura Viers for *case/lang/viers* – a wondrous alt-rock album, their registers and tones darting high and flying low like swallows before summer rain.

k.d. lang

WHEN SIGUR RÓS BEAMED DOWN THEIR SOPHOMORE LONGPLAYER *ÁGÆTIS BYRJUN* (1999) FROM THE WORLD'S NORTHERNMOST CAPITAL, ICELAND'S REYKJAVÍK, CRITICS TRIPPED OVER TO LAUD IT AS THE ONE OF THE GREAT ALBUMS OF THE CENTURY.

Singer Jónsi (b. Jón þór Birgisson; 23 April 1975) fronted the band's epic post rock, drawing a cello bow across the strings of his electric guitar, floating in and out of his soaring falsetto, singing either in Icelandic or his own made-up Hopelandic.

For all the praise of the ethereal, Jónsi's workman-like approach to his art was, in part, borne from his sexuality. His family upbringing, whilst loving, was from a hardy stock of three generations of blacksmiths. His teenage years were filled with the all too common themes of confusion and unrequited love for straight friends. Growing up in the countryside in one of the world's most sparsely populated countries, creativity was an escape from his physical and emotional isolation, fuelling his impetus to make music.

From the onset, Jónsi's sexuality was presented as a matter of fact to his fans, as it had been with his band members. While the expansive nature of Sigur Rós's music acts as a canvas on which many project their own thoughts and feelings, the band didn't fail to push creative and cultural boundaries. The video for 'Viðrar Vel Til Loftárása' (1999), featured two boys kissing on the football field, broken up by one of their fathers. Later, they captured the innocence and joy of youthful naturism (both straight and gay) in the video for 'Gobbledigook' (2008).

A decade into Sigur Rós's career Jónsi presented a solo album, *Go* (2010). Reconnecting with his youth, Jónsi ruminated (for the first time in English) around simpler times: first love, friendships and the transience of beauty, all sewn into fluttering, whistling soundscapes.

JÓNSI

WHILE HER WILFULLY WAYWARD FASHIONS AND EFFERVESCENT HITS ARE ALREADY LEGENDARY, CYNDI LAUPER'S (B. CYNTHIA ANN STEPHANIE LAUPER; 22 JUNE 1953) TIRELESS CAMPAIGNING FOR LGBTQ+ RIGHTS AND HANDS-ON SUPPORT FOR THE GAY COMMUNITY RANK HER HIGH IN THE ICON ECHELONS.

Becoming involved in gay rights advocacy because of her passion for equality, Lauper's commercial success has been a springboard from which she's carried out tireless charity work and promoted LGBTQ+ rights.

Her playful self-expression and inclusive spirit struck a chord with gay fans since the opening bounce of 'Girls Just Want To Have Fun' (1983). The track 'True Colors' (1986) resonated deeper again, its healing words of of gentle encouragement touching many during the hardest years of the AIDS crisis. The het up 'She Bop' (1984) was a pop paean to getting off, the only chart smash to namecheck gay porn in its lyrics. 'Above The Clouds' (2005) was a tribute to gay youth Matthew Shepard, whose murder called for change around hate crime legislation in the US.

Lauper's vocal delivery is wonderous: from the open highway melancholy of 'I Drove All Night' (1987) to the yearning 'Time After Time' (1984), where she gently slips away from the microphone, like a vapour trail into the ether.

Lauper's 'True Colors' tours have promoted messages of understanding and tolerance, bringing together the best LGBTQ+ musicians and allies, and raising funds for the Human Rights Campaign. Her other drives have called upon straight supporters to get involved in LGBTQ+ rights, to setting up the True Colors Residence in Harlem to provide support and shelter for LGBTQ+ homelessness.

CYNDI LAUPER

FOR TWELVE CALAMITOUS MONTHS, FRANKIE GOES TO HOLLYWOOD RULED THE 80S POP PILE. BASKING IN CONTROVERSY, BOMBASTIC HITS AND MOUNTAINS OF SLOGAN-BASED MERCHANDISE, THEIR CAREER WAS BRILLIANTLY BRIGHT AND EQUALLY SHORTLIVED.

Frankie was fronted by the defiant Holly Johnson (b. William Johnson, 9 Feb. 1960). Self-christened in homage to transgender Warholian ingenue Holly Woodlawn, from the earliest age Johnson understood pop's power to shock and thrill.

He first played bass with Big in Japan (best remembered for their various members enjoying more success with other projects). With their demise rose Frankie, who signed to producer Trevor Horn's ZTT records. He took Johnson's 'Relax' (1983), a paen to delaying sexual climax, and turned it into a tightly sprung, leather and latex beast of a song.

After an appearance on *Top of the Pops*, 'Relax' drew the ire of the BBC's censors who banned it, creating such hot demand for the song that it topped the charts for five weeks, going on to be one of the biggest songs in chart history. The nihilistic 'Two Tribes' (1984) followed, a nine week number one stayer (with 'Relax' sitting behind it at number two), and 'The Power of Love' (1984), their take on a big ballad, hitting the top for a week in December.

With these dizzy peaks came the inevitable crash, with follow-up album *Liverpool* (1986) and its singles failing to make anyway near the same impression on pop's consciousness. Frankie promptly imploded, and after a painful extrication from ZZT, Johnson re-emerged with the chipper number one album of his own, *Blast!* (1989).

After his excellent autobiography, *A Bone in My Flute* (1994), Johnson largely retreated from pop. He's still remembered as defiantly out and proud, a balls-out provocateur at a time when many other gay pop stars felt compelled to remain amongst the shadows.

HOLLY JOHNSON

FOR THE FOUR DECADES PET SHOP BOYS HAVE BEEN IN THE CHARTS, THEY'VE REVOLUTIONISED POP AS WE KNOW IT. SMACK BANG INTO THE MID-80S, WHEN CHART TOPPERS WERE ALL ABOUT MORE: THE PEARLIEST WHITES, THE BIGGEST CHORUSES, THE RAZZIEST VIDEOS, ALONG CAME NEIL AND CHRIS TO RAIN ON THE HIT PARADE.

Neil Tennant (b. 10 July 1954) (journalist at best pop weekly of all time, *Smash Hits*) and architect-to-be Chris Lowe (b. 4 Oct. 1959) met by chance in an electronics shop and quickly nerded out on all things pop, their shared tastes ranging from relentless Hi-NRG early hip hop.

Pet Shop Boys were the anti-pop pop dream, somewhere between the precise robotics of Kraftwerk and the art-as-pop of Sparks. Glum and Glummer, the hilarious underplay of their early performances became part of the PSB DNA, Tennant, he of choirboy-hued vocals, gives leaping about on stage a miss. Lowe, not un-fond of stabbing at a synthesizer with one digit, sports oversized outerwear and out-there sunglasses, expressionless.

With a couple of re-releases, their single 'West End Girls' (1984) (like Grandmaster Flash's 'The Message' (1982) reimagined in Westminster) shuffled up to dizzying chart peaks and so began what Neil coined their 'Imperial Phase': mind-bogglingly brilliant smashes that pushed pop's boundaries, moving the heart, the mind and the body, sometimes all at once.

While Tennant came out in 1994 it opened up new insight into a decade's worth of material. From early in their career they collaborated with visual artists and performers whose creative output spoke the gay community, whether writing restorative hits for the likes of Dusty Springfield and Liza Minnelli, to shooting videos with influential directors such as Derek Jarman and Bruce Weber.

In the face of the AIDS crisis of the early 90s their pop-house cover of Village People's 'Go West' (1993), backed by a broadway men's choir, is as moving as it is uplifting. The underrated 'Being Boring' (1990), nostalgic for days with friends now lost, stands about as close to pop perfection as it gets.

PET SHOP BOYS

THE RHYTHMIC GUITAR CHOPS THAT OPEN DIANA ROSS'S DIANA (B. 26 MARCH 1944) 'I'M COMING OUT' (1980) DANCE LIKE SUNBEAMS PARTING THE CLOUDS. A DECADE INTO HER SOLO CAREER SHE TOOK A GAMBLE ON A DISCO TRACK, THE GENRE THAT HAD RAPIDLY FALLEN OUT OF FAVOUR THE YEAR BEFORE.

The song's producers and songwriters Nile Rodgers and Bernard Edwards (from the legendary outfit Chic) had written the track in reaction to Chicago's Disco Demolition Night, where disco records were blown up to cheers from a straight white audience who, by association, thumbed their noses at the originators of the genre, the LGBTQ+, black and Latino communities.

Rodgers and Edwards had also just seen a nightclub full of drag impersonators, channeling Ross's various looks throughout the years. From the Supreme's earliest days (12 peerless number ones, bittersweet songs of joy and heartache), Ross was the living personification of glamour and beauty. From her sweet side-swept bob, the beehive wigs, and sequins of the 60s to her bell bottoms, and larger than life hair of the 70s, her ever-changing looks represented fierce flawlessness and inspiration for the drag community.

Despite the disco backlash, the sheer positivity of 'I'm Coming Out' was a huge hit worldwide, and the album from whence it came, *Diana* (1980) the biggest selling of her career.

While 'I'm Coming Out' is now widely recognized as a gay anthem, you could run a finger over any point of her career and find moments that resonated with her LGBTQ+ audience: from her Academy Award nominated triumph over adversity turn as Billie Holiday in *Lady Sings The Blues* (1972), the extended sexy slink of her first disco hit 'Love Hangover' (1976), to the ridiculously campy hit 'Muscles' (1982), a physique-worshipping ode written by Michael Jackson (the video featuring a nightie-clad Ross with a coterie of oiled up hunks in bikini briefs). Even 'Chain Reaction' (1985), a single harking back to the heyday sound of The Supremes, just screams extra, its seemingly endless ascent of key changes lighting up like a stairway to heaven.

DIANA ROSS

★★ QUEER ICON ★★

FRANKIE KNUCKLES (B. FRANCIS NICHOLLS; 18 JAN. 1955 – D. 31 MARCH 2014) CALLED HOUSE MUSIC 'DISCO'S REVENGE'.

For Knuckles the disco backlash of 1979 was a moment of musical reinvention. He'd moved to Chicago from New York's club scene in 1977, taking residency at gay nightclub The Warehouse, where he experimented with re-editing dancefloor cuts, underpinning them with electronic kick drums and looping polyphonic synth lines.

'House' was the sound that Knuckles built, a term coined by fans of his raise-the-roof sets, filled with constant peaks and relentless energy. Directly inspired by his sets, local producers passed on their music for him to spin, including Jamie Principal, with whom Knuckles would collaborate with on several seminal cuts including 'Your Love' (1984).

By the late 80s house music had become an international currency, and Knuckles its Godfather, lending his signature touch to remixes of household names, as well as penning underground hits of his own, the best known being 'The Whistle Song' (1991). In 1998 Knuckles was awarded the first ever Grammy in the category of Best Remixed Recording.

In 2004 Barack Obama, then a senator, renamed South Jefferson Street, where the Warehouse originally stood, Frankie Knuckles Way, and named 25 August as Frankie Knuckles Day in Chicago. Throughout his career Knuckles had worked Chicago's charities dealing with AIDS, homelessness, and youth education.

Whilst on tour in 2014, Knuckes passed away suddenly due to complications with Type 2 Diabetes. In remembering Knuckles, Barack and Michelle Obama put it succinctly: 'Frankie's work helped open minds and bring people together. He was a trailblazer in his field, and his legacy lives on in the city of Chicago and on dance floors across the globe.'

FRANKIE KNUCKLES

Armatrading moved from St Kitts in the West Indies to Birmingham in the UK when she was seven. Her parents had emigrated four years earlier and had sent for Armatrading and her siblings when they could afford to. Having tinkered on her mother's piano as a child, Armatrading taught herself guitar on an acoustic her mum had swapped for a couple of prams.

Having had to quit school at 15 in order to help support her family, her brother put her forward to play a gig at Birmingham University. Although crushingly shy, her relationship with her own songs imbued her with the confidence to perform. By the time she was 18 she'd decamped to London, performing in quintessential 60s musical *Hair!* (she refused to strip down for the show's infamous nude scenes).

She and fellow cast member Pam Nestor started writing songs together. Armatrading's vocals, however, drew her out to the front, and their songs were released under her own name for her 1972 debut *Whatever's for Us*.

She scored a bona fide hit with 'Love and Affection' (1976) which ranged from delicate emotion to punchy and rhythmic in delivery. Many of her lyrics eschewed gender pronouns, leaving both her beauties and their beholders open to interpretation by her listeners.

In the 80s she opted for a trio of all out pop albums, bearing some real chart bangers like 'Drop The Pilot' (1983) and 'Me Myself I' (1980). Amongst it all, she presented just as Joan, without make-up, bopping about in her own garms.

With twenty albums, Armatrading is a national treasure; an out musician who, while fiercely private, speaks profoundly of the human condition through her work.

JOAN ARMATRADING

FOR A PLUMP, MONOBROWED CHILD, GEORGE MICHAEL'S (GEORGIOS KYRIACOS PANAYIOTOU; B. 25 JUNE 1963 – D. 25 DEC. 2016) QUEST FOR POP STARDOM SEEMED UNLIKELY.

Working hard at his craft throughout his teens, Michael (now with two eyebrows and curtain rails for earrings) and school chum Andrew Ridgeley made it big as Wham!, teenybopper favourites, songs as sunny as their images.

Releasing two whoppingly successful Wham! albums in two years, *Fantastic* (1983) and *Make it Big* (1984), Michael yearned to stretch his creative wings. First outings *sans* Ridgeley, 'Careless Whisper' (1984) and 'A Different Corner' (1986), leaned towards a sophisticated adult sound, but debut solo album, 1987's *Faith*, lunged straight for the pop aorta.

Faith's imagery bellowed 'I am straight' from the rooftops, with Michael clad in leather and faded denim, his bum wiggling like nobody's business. *Faith* sold by the gazillion-load, and catapulted him to mega-stardom, but behind closed doors Michael was struggling with his sexuality and tiring of the game.

Divorcing himself from his image, Michael followed up with *Listen Without Prejudice Vol. 1* (1990), refusing to appear in any marketing and setting him at loggerheads with his record company. Michael found love with fashion designer Anselmo Feleppa, only to lose him to an AIDS-related brain haemorrhage, and then his mother to cancer shortly thereafter.

After a depressive spell, Michael returned with the sophisticated and touching *Older* (1996). Michael had found love again, living in LA with strapping Texan Kenny Goss, but his sexuality was outed in extraordinary style, when in 1998 he was arrested for cruising an LA park bathroom.

An absolute trooper, Michael took it squarely on the chin with the brilliant, celebratory single 'Outside' (1998). Now an openly gay man, he no longer felt beheld to sanitise his sexuality for a straight audience.

Michael's last decade was filled more with skirmishes with the law and tabloid spats than new music. Passing away unexpectedly on Christmas Day 2016, Michael left behind a legacy of amazing pop hits, stellar live performances and legions of devastated fans.

GEORGE MICHAEL

IT SEEMED LIKE DAVID BOWIE WAS A LIGHT THAT WOULD NEVER GO OUT.

The surprise release of his final album, *Blackstar* (2016), and his death two days later, seemed like an artfully staged farewell. Bowie had gripped fans in a tight bond, all the way through to the end.

As alter-ego Ziggy Stardust for 'The Rise and Fall of Ziggy Stardust and the Spiders from Mars' (1972) Bowie had rebirthed from 'kinda interesting' to alien androgyne, a look and persona that flipped masculinity on its head and blew people's minds. 'I'm gay,' he informed *Melody Maker*, 'and always have been'.

In his performance of 'Starman' (1972) on *Top of the Pops*, Bowie draped his arm over guitarist Mick Ronson's frame, locking eyes and in turn unlocking the minds of millions of captive viewers. Some were scandalised (a man touching a man? Perish the thought!), but for other thousands of disenfranchised youth – gay, straight or otherwise – a message beamed from the TV screen and into their hearts: 'you are OK'.

Bowie was an instigator of 'other'. Full of contradictions, he was married with a child but told the press he was gay. He used gay vernacular to colour his own songs ('The Jean Genie' (1972), 'Queen Bitch' (1971)) and to touch some of the best work of others (Lou Reed's queer fairytale 'Walk On The Wild Side' (1972)). The sassy coquette of 'John, I'm Only Dancing' (1972) was so outré risqué that the US didn't release it until it was a four year old, in 1976.

His wham, bam, thank you glam zinged up the UK's straight rockers to get razzy with glitter and boas. The video for 'DJ' (1979) saw him beleaguered by fans, kissed full on the mouth by a male passerby. 'Boys Keep Swinging' (1979) was an array of Bowies in drag of all ages. 'Ashes to Ashes' (1980) was Bowie as pop's fairy godfather, ordaining the soon to be New Romantic scene; heroes of the 80s to pass through pop's hallowed halls with his blessing.

The door swung both ways. The 'gay' tag served Bowie well, as it in turn, served his fans. Blurring lines, in music, art and his sexuality, Bowie planted seeds from which many fabulous children would grow.

DAVID BOWIE

★★ QUEER ICON ★★

FROM HUMBLE BEGINNINGS AS ESSEX'S REGINALD DWIGHT, ELTON JOHN (B. 25 MARCH 1947) FOUND HIS WAY IN THE WORLD OF MUSIC, MOVING THROUGH CLASSICAL PIANO (WINNING A SCHOLARSHIP TO THE ROYAL ACADEMY OF MUSIC AGE 11) TO PURSUING A DREAM OF MAKING IT IN SHOW BUSINESS.

With songwriting partner Bernie Taupin, Elton RULED the 70s, invading charts and airwaves with a golden marathon of 25 top forty, 16 top ten, and six number one hits.

The duo's on-point formula, flipping between gospel-chorded rockers and poignant ballads, made John the hottest act in rock 'n' roll. By the mid-70s he was filling stadiums and donning outrageous stagewear. His extravagant public image (Donald Duck outfits, sequinned baseball uniforms, $40,000 loon glasses) belied his personal struggles. After revealing his bisexuality in 1976 to *Rolling Stone*, he was hounded by the press, announcing an early retirement in 1977.

He returned in the 80s with some decent to middling hits and bizarre choices in his personal life, surprising press and public when he married studio engineer Renate Blauel. His vices of the 70s, cocaine and alcohol, as well as his difficulty reconciling himself with the unhappy child he'd once been loomed heavily over him.

In the 90s, John went public with his personal demons, and turned a corner. He lost weight, got a fetching new barnet, and upped sticks to Atlanta, Georgia. In 1992, he founded the Elton John AIDS Foundation, donating all future royalties from his single sales of to AIDS research.

In 1997 he was rocked by the sudden deaths of two of his close friends, designer Gianni Versace and Princess Diana. A reworked version of his 1973 song 'Candle in the Wind', with all proceeds donated to the Diana, Princess of Wales Memorial Fund, outsold all of his other singles combined.

Having enjoyed a 20-plus year relationship (now marriage) with David Furnish and with two young sons, John remains prolific, outspoken, generous and human.

ELTON JOHN

WITH A PATCHWORK CAREER, SKITTERING FOR MORE THAN FIFTY YEARS ACROSS MUSIC, FILM AND THEATRE, JAYNE COUNTY (B. WAYNE ROGERS; 1947) HAS RATTLED CAGES. A TRUE PROVOCATEUR AND ONE (IF NOT THE FIRST) OF ROCK'S EARLIEST TRANSGENDER FIGURES.

Born and raised in the less permissive climate of Georgia, Alabama, by his early teens self-proclaimed sissy-boy Wayne was experimenting with drag and make-up. While escaping to New York appeared a relative refuge, even within the hippy enclave of the West Village, County was caught up in the now legendary Stonewall Riots of 1969.

After schlubbing it out in boring day jobs, County fell in with two of Warhol's Factory superstars, the shiny drag queens Holly Woodlawn and Jackie Curtis. Curtis encouraged County to embrace a more extravagant, absurdist approach to cross-dressing. Soon enough County had moved onto stage, performing in surrealist theatrical performances and DJing at New York counterculture hangout du jour, Max's Kansas City.

By 1972 County was fronting rock band Queen Elizabeth, their raunchy and outrageous stage antics catching the attention of David Bowie's management company, MainMan. They dropped a fortune on filming County's experimental theatre show 'Wayne at the Trucks', but its release never saw the light of day.

Undeterred, as Wayne County and the Backstreet Boys, they carried on, regular fixtures on New York's emerging proto punk scene. With The Sex Pistols and The Clash becoming household names, County had begun to develop a following in Europe. At this time Wayne began her transition to Jayne, making her not only the first trans rock star, but transforming under the full glare of the public eye.

An appetite for amphetamines and tensions within County's band meant that her recording career largely imploded by the decade's end. Nevertheless, songs such as 'Fuck Off' (1977) and 'Man Enough To Be a Woman' (1986) go some way to capturing her ability to amuse, titillate and revile in equal measures.

JAYNE COUNTY

SURROUNDED BY MUSICAL ROYALTY (GODMOTHER ARETHA FRANKLIN, COUSIN DIONNE WARWICK), WITH STUNNING LOOKS AND A POWERHOUSE VOICE, WHITNEY HOUSTON (B. 9 AUG. 1963 – D. 11 FEB. 2012) SEEMED DESTINED TO BE A BLINDINGLY SUCCESSFUL ENTERTAINER.

Despite her incredible wealth and accolades, Houston was seemed always on the outside looking in at her career. An African-American woman strong-armed by record label to 'toned down' her blackness to be more 'palatable' to the record buying public. A woman confused by her sexuality, unsupported by her family and pushed to maintain a straight image for the sake of her career. A talent corroded away by an entourage of hangers-on and opportunists.

Houston's voice was a showstopper, able to tackle everything from the slushiest of ballads to the most effervescent pop tunes. Combined with her fresh-faced beauty she was groomed to be an international crossover superstar and she delivered, going global on her first two albums with everything from the late-night jazzy 'Saving All My Love For You' (1985) to the giddy 'So Emotional' (1987) and 'I Wanna Dance With Somebody' (1987). Even these early pop confections portended to darker waters, her nuanced performances hinting at fear of rejection alongside side hopeful daydreaming.

Her cover of Dolly Parton's 'I Will Always Love You' (1992) from the film *The Bodyguard*, and its accompanying soundtrack broke new records. From up here at the peak of success, Houston would spend much of the remainder of her short life trying to unshackle herself from it.

As a vocalist Houston became THE standard to which R&B vocalists would, and continue to aspire. At every stage of her career it was all about the voice; the conduit that allowed her to express her own personal hopes, betrayals and disappointments, irrespective of the material or genre.

WHITNEY HOUSTON

★★ QUEER ICON ★★

Sexually active and identifying as gay from an early age, Sylvester experienced rejection from both his church and family, effectively being made homeless. He moved into the fold of the Disquotays, a collective of fearless black transgender women and crossdressers, defiantly at odds with the world around them, hosting wild happenings in some of Los Angeles' most conservative black neighbourhoods.

In the early 70s, Sylvester was beckoned to the free love counterculture of San Francisco. He fell in with The Cockettes, a bawdy troupe of Gay Lib hippies, whose late night revue, hallucinatory-fuelled bearded drag, was a thing of local legend. Sylvester's elegant drag and creamy falsetto, performing the torch songs of idols such as Billie Holiday, brought some welcome chiaroscuro to The Cockettes' kaleidoscopic cacophony.

The Cockettes imploded after a much anticipated (and deeply disastrous) debut performance in New York in 1971. After a few years in the rock wilderness called Sylvester. Disco fit him like a glove. The percolating, contagious, 'You Make Me Feel (Mighty Real)' (1978) was the perfect musical foil for Sylvester's spiritual, gospel informed singing and his besquinned, glamazonian appearance. Sylvester's hits encapsulated the best of disco and the ebullience of San Francisco's gay life, before the AIDS crisis of the early 80s drew a long, dark shadow over the city.

Sylvester died from complications arising from AIDS in 1988, bequeathing all future royalties from his music to San Francisco-based HIV/AIDS charities. To this day the relentless Hi-NRG of 'You Make Me Feel (Mighty Real)', and 'Do You Wanna Funk' (1982) continue to bring people of all backgrounds together on the dance floor.

SYLVESTER

FROM SANDPIT PLAYMATES TO STADIUM PERFORMERS, OLIVER SIM AND ROMY MADLEY CROFT HAVE BEEN JOINED AT THE HIP THEIR ENTIRE LIVES. WITH JAMIE SMITH BROUGHT INTO THEIR FOLD AGED 11, COLLECTIVELY THEY MAKE UP THE xx.

They formed The xx in their final year of school, pooling together demos in a South London garage. Not having much idea what to do with their music, they posted some demos online (to little avail), they dropped some music to their label Young Turks and subsequently found themselves signed at the end of their teens.

The distinct intimacy of their sound reflected the shared bond of their formative years together. Built around the dual carriageway of Croft and Sim's unadorned, quietly soulful vocals, and Smith's subtle electronics, the band's sound – while drawing from both alternative rock and a subtle R&B shuffle – was a palette cleanser for many jaded ears, like whispered musical pillow talk in an age of bombastic popstar excess.

Critics and fans bought in to their single 'Crystalised' (2009). Their debut *xx* (2009), a collection of understated love songs, clocked up a million sales around the world and scooped the Mercury Prize in 2010. The xx were now indie darlings. Forever donning their signature black, their record sleeves and artwork taking minimal to the max.

Over the next couple of years Sim and Croft both worked through issues, changes and tragedies within their family dynamics, emerging through this with their second album, *Coexist* (2012), and later the energised, less lugubrious *I See You* (2017).

Joining the ranks with other queer musicians (Sim and Croft are both gay), The xx are out, yet not overly political, performing in an age and to an audience for whom their definition of sexuality is perhaps less important, or relevant. The crafted intimacy, however, is relatable from both a queer and universal perspective alike.

The xx

FREDDIE MERCURY (B. FARROKH BULSARA; 5 SEPT. 1946 – D. 24 NOV. 1991), QUITE POSSIBILITY ZANZIBAR'S MOST FAMOUS EXPORT, IS RECOGNISED AS THE QUINTESSENTIAL ROCK PERFORMER. AN INTRIGUING MIX OF INTENSE PRIVACY AND MUSIC ABILITY, ON STAGE MERCURY CAME ALIVE LIKE AN ELECTRIFIED COCKEREL, FULL OF STRUT AND SWAGGER.

Moving to London in his teens, Mercury formed Queen in 1970, combining unlikely musical styles (operetta and glam rock, anyone?) to produce two decades of back to back rock smashes. A vocal virtuoso and a canny lyricist, Queen ruled the airwaves and sold albums by the bucketload. To this day, their performance at Live Aid in 1985 is lauded by many as the best rock performance of all time.

Mercury's persona in Queen toyed with many dress codes that were hitherto unrecognised by their largely straight audience – his splendiferous moustache (once voted Britain's best), leather gear, glove-like fitted white vests bristling with chest hair – all spoke 'gay' if you were in the know. The 1984 video for 'I Want To Break Free' saw Mercury and the band perform household chores in suburban drag, Mercury's signature moustache intact.

Although stating early in this career, 'I'm as gay as a daffodil, my dear', Mercury's personal life was an endless source of speculation for the press and public. While unafraid to display his sexuality, he was equally as reticent to justify or discuss his way of life. Hounded by the UK's tabloids, though Mercury had been diagnosed with HIV in 1987, it wasn't until the day before his death some four years later that he made his status known to the public.

The year after his death, Mercury was awarded the Brit Award for Outstanding Contribution to British Music. His bandmates founded The Mercury Phoenix Trust and organised The Freddie Mercury Tribute Concert for AIDS Awareness, held at Wembley, celebrating Mercury's life and legacy and raise money for AIDS research. Although Mercury's life off stage had been shrouded in privacy, in his passing he shone a huge light around AIDS awareness and its prevention.

FREDDIE MERCURY

JOBRIATH (B. BRUCE WAYNE CAMPBELL: 14 DEC. 1946 - 3 AUG. 1983) WAS THE GREATEST STAR THAT NEVER WAS.

As the dayglo dreams of 60s counterculture faded, the 70s was a hard bump back to reality. On both sides of the Atlantic, acts such as Iggy Pop, The New York Dolls, T-Rex and Roxy Music provided a sliver of sparkle in contrast to the grey drudgery of every life.

The stage was set for Jobriath, a gap-toothed, hippy pouter with sizeable abilities as vocalist, pianist and performer. As Wolf in the late-60s production of *Hair!*, Jobriath's talents soon came into the tractor beam of charismatic manager Jerry Brandt.

Brandt saw dollar signs in a new type of global superstar, an uber Ziggy Stardust. Brandt hyped Jobriath into a record label mega-deal, and in the months ahead of his debut eponymous LP (1973), an over-the-top marketing campaign splashed Jobriath across billboards, buses and magazines. No one bought in. *Jobriath*, despite its inventive mix of baroque pop, musical theatre and glam rock, didn't even chart.

Jobriath's public declaration as 'the true fairy of rock' rankled with music journalists. Unlike Bowie, Jobriath was not in character. The gay community, heading into an era of butch realness, shunned him, embarrassed by his OTT presentation.

A tour of the Opera Houses of Europe was announced, which was reduced to a typical band-in-van schlub around venues in the US. A live performance on US rock TV show *The Midnight Special* fizzed, appearing small scale, confusing and sad. His second album *Creatures of the Street* (1974) received no marketing, or attention, and Jobriath was unceremoniously dropped from his label.

Jobriath quietly reinvented as cabaret crooner Cole Berlin, working New York's hotel piano bar circuit. Lean times saw him carve out another career as Joby, an oiled up hustler for rent.

Jobriath was one of the first pop stars to die from an AIDS-related illness. While forgotten to a wider audience, champions such as Morrissey and Marc Almond continue to shine a light on his real, overlooked talents.

JOBRIATH

FOR SO MANY PEOPLE, CHER (B.CHERILYN SARKISIAN; 20 MAY 1946) IS, IN HERSELF, A CAUSE FOR CELEBRATION. WITH HER BURNISHED CARAMEL CONTRALTO, HER ABILITY TO HONE IN ON MUSICAL TRENDS AND HER EVER-EVOLVING APPEARANCE, CHER'S SIX DECADES IN THE CHARTS HAVE BEEN NOTHING SHORT OF INCREDIBLE.

A lanky brunette in an era of blonde bombshells, Cher hit LA's Sunset Strip in the early 60s, hoping to unlock her ambitions for fame and success. Sonny Bono, shorter in stature and higher in vocal range, was the key. From friends, to lovers, to pop duo, they made it super big with the 'I Got You Babe' (1965).

Through TV show *The Sonny and Cher Comedy Hour* Cher became a bona fide star. It was the perfect platform to propel massive hits like 'Gypsys, Tramps & Thieves' (1971), and 'Dark Lady' (1974) straight to the top of the charts. Her outrageous wardrobe – from zany to racy – was as popular as her songs, peppering the mind of many a young drag queen with outrageous looks to aspire to.

After divorcing Sonny and a short lived, ill-advised marriage with bluesman Greg Allman, the 70s drew a close, and Cher regained the pop crown with a slinky Disco hit, 'Take Me Home' (1979).

Most of the 80s saw Cher's eye on the acting prize, culminating in an Oscar for Best Actress for 1987's *Moonstruck* and a hit with a cutesy cover of Rudy Clark's 60s hit 'The Shoop Shoop Song (It's in His Kiss)'. Before the decade was over Cher switched it up with 'Turn Back Time (1989), entering her scantily clad, cannon-straddling phase, a power ballad MILF belting out soft-centred smashes to randy sailors and raucous cowboys.

The unforgettable autotune wibble of 98's 'Believe' (1998) re-invented Cher again, as positivity-through adversity dance-pop queen; the song, a two-time Grammy winning earworm that informed dance music vocals for the next decade.

Seemingly ageless (her forays into plastic surgery only seem to make her more Cher), Cher's hard won success looks set to be embraced by the LGBTQ+ community for years to come.

CHER

★★ QUEER ICON ★★

JOHN GRANT'S SUCCESS (B. 25 JULY 1968) ARRIVED AT A TIME WHEN MANY OTHERS WOULD BE CONSIDERED PAST THEIR COMMERCIAL SELL-BY DATE.

Growing up in Colorado against a backdrop of daily homophobia, music was an outlet and an escape. Grant's natural flair for language gave him an out, allowing him to move to Germany to study. Unfortunately, his debilitating anxieties chased him there, and on news of his mother's ailing health, he returned home.

With his mother's passing, Grant weaved through prescription drugs, hitting the bottle and caning it on class As. He formed a band, The Czars, who produced six albums, finding some acclaim and next to no commercial success. Eventually even his bandmates were jack of his trainwreck behaviour and in 2006 The Czars called it a day.

Music seemed done for Grant, he joined AA and moved East to New York, working as an interpreter in hospitals. Folk rock band Midlake provided a musical lifeline, encouraging Grant to head to Texas and work them for what would become *Queen of Denmark* (2010), his debut longplayer.

Queen Of Denmark was a remarkable rear view look at Grant's rite of passage as a gay youth lost in the Midwest. His lyrical wit and handsome baritone (he could sing from a takeaway menu and make it sound good), cocooned in Midlake's warm, tender arrangements, led to the album being quietly hailed as an instant classic.

The UK in particular warmed to Grant's considerable charms, a career in music finally becoming an actuality. Tinged with subtle electronic flourishes *Pale Green Ghosts* (2013), again traced his past, but with a sharper focus to a relationship awry. *Grey Tickles, Black Pressure* (2015) saw Grant shift from his past to an angier, belligerant present.

In 2011 Grant revealed his HIV positive status whilst on stage. It seemed the right place, for Grant his life and music are inextricably linked.

JOHN GRANT

ERASURE'S ANDY BELL (B. 25 APRIL 1964) PLUCKED HIMSELF FROM OBSCURITY BY RESPONDING TO AN AD IN THE NOW DEFUNCT MUSIC RAG *MELODY MAKER*.

Musical serial dater Vince Clarke (who'd written and produced Depeche Mode's biggest hits, before forming short-lived gutsy electronic duo Yazoo with Basildon bellower Alison Moyet) sought a vocalist for his new project. Neither of them were to know this next musical journey, Erasure, would go on to sell over 25 million albums.

Bell's early vocal forays could be summed up into two words: 'Alison' and 'Moyet', yet as he eased into the process his voice took full flight along with his songwriting, the perfect foil to Vince's synth pop confections. Erasure knew the lane they were driving in – and after a slow start – they produced hit after hit, over 40 of them in fact.

Out in a time when most gay musicians would, at best, allude obliquely to their sexuality, Bell was completely unapologetic for who he was, refusing to play straight roles in videos or change his lyrics to be more palatable to a straight market. While offstage Bell was shy, his onstage persona was anything but – part pantomime dame, part go-go dancer. One deliciously over the top tour after another witnessed everything from Bell's pert assets bouncing in backless rhinestone chaps, to casually straddling an enormous penis on stage.

While Erasure's huge following were sometimes strangely oblivious to his camp excesses, in 1992 they went stratospheric in the UK with their *Abba-eqsue* EP – riding the crest of a wave that would introduce a new generation to Sweden's fabbest four.

Life in the spotlight wasn't without its difficult moments – losing his longtime partner and manager, Paul M. Hickey, two hip replacements and, in 2004, revealing his HIV status in what was still a frosty tabloid climate in the UK.

Though all of this, with Clarke (a working relationship spanning four decades) Bell's continued to deliver music full of unbridled enthusiasm – passionate, wide-eyed and sincere. Mr Bell, we salute you.

ANDY BELL

FOR YEARS LADY GAGA (B. STEFANI JOANNE ANGELINA GERMANOTTA; 28 MARCH 1986) PACED IT OUT THROUGH PRIVATE CONVENT SCHOOL REBELLION, MUSIC TUITION, ACTING SCHOOL AND AN OBLIGATORY LOWER EAST SIDE 'SLUMMING IT' PHASE. WHEN THE CROSSOVER FINALLY KICKED OFF WITH 'JUST DANCE', SHE WASTED NO TIME IN ACKNOWLEDGING THE EARLY SUPPORT OF HER LGBTQ+ FANBASE.

Frothy pop earworms, topped with an everything-and-two-kitchen-sinks dress sense and razzy, slick music videos made Gaga an obvious pick for your Friday night on the tiles. As success quickly mounted with some stonkingly poptastic singles, Gaga took on the mantle as one of the LGBTQ+ community's fiercest advocates.

Coming out as bisexual in 2009, Gaga joined the National Equality March to the White House in support of LGBTQ+ rights. As well as making uncooked sirloin a new red carpet look at the 2010 MTV Video Music Awards, she also brought with her former gay and lesbian US soldiers who hadn't been able to serve openly under the military's policy at the time.

2011's 'Born This Way' her 'this-is-who-the-fuck-I-am' anthem, was lyrically overt celebration of the sexual spectrum and individuality. Its energy – somewhere between the disco ebullience of Patrick Hernandez's 'Born to Be Alive' (1979) and the women-on-top, can-do positivity of Madonna's 'Express Yourself' (1989) – imbued her life-as-art and vice versa philosophy. On the back of the single she launched the Born This Way Foundation, launching initiatives to end the bullying of LGBTQ+ youth.

Despite the uber-hooky songs, Gaga's catchy kookiness was shocking yet somehow expected. At her peak, she brought the story of her LGBTQ+ fans with her to centre stage. Here's hoping her Las Vegas residency sees her return to pop's throne.

LADY GAGA

★★ QUEER ICON ★★

IN THE AGE OF MEMES, ONE OF LIBERACE'S (LIBERACE WŁADZIU VALENTINO LIBERACE; B. 16 MAY 1919 – D. 4 FEB. 1987) STAGE ENTRANCES, GLIDING IN ON A WIRE TRAPEZE, WAS GAME TO BE CUT AND SPLICED FOR LOLS. 'THE FLOOR IS HETEROSEXUALITY!' SCREAMED THE MEME AS LIBERACE FLIES THROUGH AIR, DROWNING IN FUR CAPE AND JEWELS.

Thirty years after his death, the contradictions of Liberace's life can be prodded without fear of litigious recrimination. While Liberace out-plumed a peacock, he never publicly acknowledged his homosexuality, and did everything to throw his adoring public – the housewives of middle America – off the scent.

Born into a musical yet conservative working-class household, Liberace was playing the piano by age four. By seven he'd joined the Wisconsin College of Music, and was performing with orchestras in his early teens.

He found success blending schmaltzy classics with pop music. When he found his way onto TV sets in the 50s with *The Liberace Hour*, his ivory tinkling drew a weekly audience of up to 30 million viewers. Las Vegas fit Liberace like a glove, and he entered a series of long-standing residencies, becoming one of the world's wealthiest entertainers. Night after night he performed at his candelabra-topped grand piano, dripping in an endless array of sartorial excess.

His onstage persona was about as sexy as a glass of milk, deliberately put together to be as un-threatening as possible. 'Mr Showmanship' was militant in maximising his public appeal, and that included shooting down allusions to his sexual orientation. He set up a long string of 'beards' – friendships and romantic links with women – to maintain a hetero status quo in the media. Articles alluding to his homosexuality were cut at the quick, Liberace suing gossip columnists so successfully that he coined the phrase 'I cried all the way to the bank!'. Even in death, due to complications from AIDS, family and friends tried to hide his sexuality from his fans.

LIBERACE

THE SYNTH SOUNDS OF BRONSKI BEAT WERE IN PART A TROJAN HORSE. PINT-SIZED FRONTMAN JIMMY SOMERVILLE (B. 22 JUNE 1961) LOOKED AS FRIENDLY AS TINTIN COME TO LIFE, BUT BRONSKI BEAT WERE ANGRY: QUEER, A VOICE IN THE CHARTS FOR THE DISENFRANCHISED YOUTH OF 80S BRITAIN.

In 1967, sex acts between two gay adults were decriminalised. Unlike the majority of Europe, Britain's age of consent for gay men remained at 21. While straight youth lay back and thought of England, young LGBTQ+ people broke the law with every sexual dalliance. In a society where they felt, at best, tolerated, the ongoing age of consent was a kick in the guts.

Bronski Beat's 'Smalltown Boy' (1984), mirrored elements of singer Jimmy Somerville's life journey, carried by his haunting signature falsetto vocals. In its video, Somerville and bandmates hang about the local swimming pool, admiring the charms of some youths. The admiration is not reciprocated, they're beaten up and Somerville is returned home by the police, admonished by his father and met with tears by his mother. He packs up and sets out alone, on what hopes to be a new life in a new town.

'Smalltown Boy' brought the shared gay experience into the charts and onto TV. Its album *Age of Consent* (1984) didn't just spark debate in the UK, it was a worldwide hit.

Somerville's relationship with Bronski Beat was short lived, and after one album Somerville was off, nailing his socialist colours to the mast with Communards, who scored 1986's biggest UK hit with 'Don't Leave Me This Way'.

With the close of the 80s and a solo album from Somerville, the less tantalising *Read My Lips* (1989) things grew quieter. Somerville remains a hero, tackling homophobia and inequality head-on in what was a turbulent era for LGBTQ+ rights.

JIMMY
SOMERVILLE

NINA SIMONE ENDS HER SONG 'FOUR WOMEN' (1966) SHOUTING OUT HER NAME IS 'PEACHES' LIKE AN ASCENDING WAR CRY. SOME 30-ODD YEARS LATER, THE MONIKER WOULD BE ADOPTED BY A CANADIAN SCHOOL TEACHER, TRANSFORMING HER FROM TORONTO'S MERRILL NISKER (B.11 NOV. 1966) TO THE ONE-WOMAN MUSICAL AND SEXUAL REVOLUTION THAT IS PEACHES.

Nisker first found her way around a guitar in the classroom, and joined a folk group, the very Phoebe-from-*Friends* named Mermaid Café. The creative limitations of a folk band soon became evident, and Merrill began bumping around with art-punk group called The Shit.

Fatiguing of Toronto, she joined pal and former The Shit member Chilly Gonzales in Berlin, where she set about creating her sexually-charged alter ego, trying together her love-hate relationship with hip hop and punk rock to her own theatrical D.I.Y. aesthetic.

Her *The Teaches of Peaches* (2000) pushed sex positivity to the fore, and its lead single 'Fuck The Pain Away' quickly gained Peaches a broad church of fans, from Björk and Iggy Pop to Britney Spears and Christina Aguilera.

She continued to blur gender lines, and sporting a full beard on the cover of for her next album *Fatherfucker* (2003). She countered the fake titties and shaved privates of porn's straight male gaze by touring a joyous live show, a sexy free-for-all featuring wildly exaggerated genitalia, mountains of pubic hair and furiously jiggling privates.

After her 2006 call to arms, *Impeach My Bush*, and the more electro-leaning *I Feel Cream* (2009) she expanded her talents to an ambitious rock opera stage show and film *Peaches Does Herself* (2012). She followed with a defiantly queer, one-woman production of *Jesus Christ Superstar*, interpolated as *Peaches Christ Superstar*.

Some 15 years into her career, her joyful sexual transgression shows no signs of abating. For the title track of her album *Rub* (2015), Peaches created a video like a queer utopia, a female fuck-for-all bordering on shamanic in its ceremonious sexual intensity.

PEACHES

★★ QUEER ICON ★★

ASK ANYONE TO NAME A CLASSIC ELVIS PRESLEY TRACK, AND 'HOUND DOG' (1952) IS ALWAYS UP THERE. MOST PEOPLE ARE UNAWARE, HOWEVER, THAT THE ORIGINAL VERSION WAS RECORDED AND RELEASED THREE YEARS EARLIER BY WILLIE MAE THORNTON (B. 11 DEC. 1926 – 25 JULY 1984), WHO SHIFTED A CHEEKY COUPLE OF MILLION COPIES AND TOPPED THE BILLBOARD CHARTS.

Born into a religious Alabama family, Thornton was precociously talented, a triple threat of gutsy vocals, drums and a mean harmonica. As a teen she cleaned up local amateur talent shows, before landing a gig with the Hot Harlem Revue, busting her chops for seven years of relentless touring schedule for the next seven years before hitting the studio.

'Big Mama' was big in voice, talent and personality. Musicians, producers and managers all learnt the hard way that Thornton was not one to be trifled with. On and off stage she donned sharp men's suits and hats – 'outrageous' at the time – and made no attempts to hide her sexual preferences, or to succumb to notions of how African-American women (or women in general) should deport themselves.

Presley and another queer icon, Janis Joplin, were ardent admirers of her blues holler, evident in their own vocal deliveries. Joplin went on to cover Big Mama's 'Ball and Chain' in 1968, again eclipsing the success of Thornton's own version.

After a fair but relatively fruitless stab at further chart success, Thornton headed to the West Coast in the early 60s. Hard living in her last years took its toll on Thornton's heart and liver. Former producer and friend Jonny Otis noted the media attention surrounding her death had been sorely lacking in her recording years. In the time since, however, Thornton's reputation as queer pioneer and rock 'n' roll innovator continues to deservedly grow.

WILLIE MAE THORNTON

FOR A GOOD DECADE AND A HALF OF THEIR 30-YEAR CAREER, MICHAEL STIPE (B. 4 JAN. 1960) AND HIS BAND R.E.M. MAPPED OUT THE PATH THAT WOULD DEFINE 'ALTERNATIVE MUSIC'.

Their first album *Murmur* (1983) drew together D.I.Y. aesthetics with hooky guitars and wilfully obscure lyrics. Despite their indie stripes the band was ambitious, toiling mercilessly to build a fanbase. With each year they refined their sound, traversing garage rock and haunting ballads, Stipe's lyrics opening up, delivered in his signature plaintive style.

'The One I Love' (1987) brought them stadium-sized performances. With the release of *Out of Time* (1991), and its singles, 'Losing My Religion', and 'Shiny Happy People', R.E.M. entered rock's mile high club, ubiquitous on radio, MTV and in college kids' record collections. *Automatic for the People* (1992) and its four singles were nothing less than gargantuan.

Success held a mirror up to an audience Stipe didn't altogether recognise. Many of their devoted fanbase, indie freaks and geeks, had been replaced by an audience whose values were in opposition to his own, many of whom would have actively disapproved of his sexuality.

In 1994 Stipe decided to come out as a queer man, standing beside a scant handful of figures in rock willing to risk fame and wealth to speak their truth. While some fans seemed unable, or unwilling, to process Stipe's news, publicly acknowledging his queerness released him from the confines of his fame, and made much of his past work seem all sweeter. The mournful nostalgia of 'Nightswimming' (1993) and swinging ache of 'Everybody Hurts' (1993) glowed, imbued with a deeper heartfelt resonance.

In his time since R.E.M., unshackled from his fame monster, Stipe does mainly whatever the fuck he wants, moving between film, art and occasionally music, all with an intuitive ease aligned with his queer outlook.

MICHAEL STIPE

FRANK OCEAN (B. CHRISTOPHER EDWIN BREAUX; 28 OCT. 1987) EPITOMISES THE NOW, A TRULY MODERN, QUEER R&B RISK-TAKER. GROWING UP IN NEW ORLEANS, OCEAN ROLLED THE DICE AND DECAMPED TO LOS ANGELES AFTER HURRICANE KATRINA HIT AND WIPED AWAY HIS STUDIO, AIMING TO MAKE IT AS A SONGWRITER.

Make it he did, writing on cuts for the likes of Beyoncé, Bieber and Brandy, as well as circling around with infamous LA hip hop pranksters Odd Future, who inspired him to pursue his own music, beginning with mixtape *Nostalgia, ULTRA* (2011).

In 2012, days before dropping his debut longplayer *Channel Orange*, Ocean posted an open letter to his Tumblr, recounting the joy and pain of falling for a another guy when he was 19. 'If I listen closely', he wrote, 'I can feel the sky falling too.'

For a moment in the hip hop and R&B world the skies did fall. *Channel Orange* became THE flash point in the conversation about homophobia in music, and in that moment Ocean drew in swathes LGBTQ+ fans. It didn't hurt either that his talents were matched by crushingly good looks and an inherent sense of style. *Channel Orange* turned over genres like pages in a book, and its heartache moments of one-sided, unrequited love for another man seared with longing.

Ocean was breaking entirely new ground for urban music. By coming to grips with his queerness through his songwriting, Ocean brought catharsis, not only for himself, but to many of his listeners.

With years of mounting anticipation, mercurial Ocean re-emerged with three projects – a visual album, *Endless* (2016), the mellifluous, *Blonde* (2016) and a luxe oversized magazine *Boys Don't Cry* (2016) that plunged further into his psyche – poems, photography, guys, cars – exploring a sensibility, like Ocean himself, that was undoubtedly queer in outlook but oblique, more show than tell.

FRANK OCEAN

WHILE PRAISED BY SOME AS SPEARHEADING THE 'QUEER RAP' MOVEMENT OF THIS DECADE MICHAEL DAVID QUATTLEBAUM JR. (B. 2 APRIL 1986), AKA MYKKI BLANCO, CAST HIS NET MUCH WIDER, A CREATIVE OMNIVORE WEARING DIFFERENT HATS AT EVERY TURN: RAPPER, PERFORMANCE ARTIST, POET, ACTIVIST AND DOCUMENTARY MAKER.

Culturally stifled in his hometown of North Carolina, as a teen he decamped to New York, testing the waters with painting, photography and performance poetry before Blanco, 'international cross-dressing It Girl', was birthed in 2010 as a video art project.

It Girl Blanco decided she wanted to stick around. As the performances began to evolve into out-of-the-box rap videos, Blanco found that people were responding to the music as much as they were to the imagery. People were calling Blanco a rapper, albeit one under a new mantle, visceral and complex, the type who was unafraid to spit quickfire freestyle on a street corner in full drag.

This rapper's influences, however, were not just hip hop, but rather a heady mix of leftfield MCs, transgressive queer artists, punk and Riot Grrrl girl. Blanco stepsided pigeonholing by releasing tracks and videos as creatively disparate as possible, from the razor's edge noise of *Mykki Blanco & the Mutant Angels* (2012) to the feminist punk hip hop of *Gay Dog Food* (2014). Blanco's videos and art performances go hand-in-hand with the music, a fast paced, flick book of evolving looks and moods, high couture and street smarts, as difficult to categorise as the music genres he plays between.

By 2015, Blanco had reached a creative impasse. Without a record label, money and or creative horizon to swim towards, he chose, with a degree of trepidation, to reveal to his fans that he was HIV positive. The warmth he received in response to his news inspired him to forge ahead on his creative path, releasing his solo longplayer *Mykki* in 2016 to great critical acclaim.

MYKKI BLANCO

GROWING UP IN PORT ARTHUR, TEXAS, JANIS JOPLIN (B. 19 JAN. 1943 - D. 4 OCT. 1970) DRIFTED THROUGH HIGH SCHOOL AS A MISFIT, PICKED ON BECAUSE OF HER LOOKS AND OPEN MINDEDNESS. MUSIC WAS HER ANCHOR, AND AFTER BEING INTRODUCED TO THE HOLLERING WONDERS OF MA RAINEY AND BESSIE SMITH, JOPLIN TESTED OUT OUT HER OWN VOICE, SINGING BLUES AND FOLK WITH FRIENDS.

University was the place for her to try on rebellion for size, Joplin modelling herself on beat poets and her blues heroines, wandering around campus barefoot in jeans. Before too long she drifted West, hitchhiking with a friend to San Francisco, where she found her feet in the Bay Area's large musical community. She also found drugs, becoming a regular user of both speed and heroin.

After a recovery stint back with her parents she returned to San Francisco's hippy scene, fronting Big Brother and the Holding Company. When the band played at Monterey Pop Festival in 1967 Joplin's success skyrocketed, her electric stage presence and unbridled vocals – bruised, soulful and free – garnered her lavish attention, creating tension between her and the rest of the band.

With their album *Cheap Thrills* (1968), a chart-topping hit, Joplin's fame reintroduced her to alcohol and drugs. Things got too tense and Joplin left to front the Kozmic Blues Band, touring Europe, scoring another hit with *I Got Dem Ol' Kozmic Blues Again Mama!* (1969) making television appearances, performing everywhere from Woodstock Festival to Madison Square Garden.

Joplin's fashions were a kaleidoplace explosion of tinted glasses, corduroys, bell bottoms and feather boas. Success brought fame, wealth, and lovers, but her inability to assimilate the star she'd become with the 'real' Joplin saw her plunge deeper into addiction. While Joplin had relationships with both men and women, she continued to run from the ridicule and humiliation she endured in her teen years. Joplin died from an accidental heroin overdose. Her final album *Pearl!* (1971), and its single 'Me and Bobby McGee' were both posthumous number ones.

JANIS JOPLIN

WHILE LONDON'S BLITZ KIDS PREENED AND FLOUNCED IN THEIR NEW ROMANTIC MICROVERSE, IN LIVERPOOL PETE BURNS (B. 5 AUG. 1959 – D. 23 OCT. 2016) STOOD ALONE, SHOCKING AND AMAZING LOCALS LONG BEFORE HE TOPPED THE GLOBAL POP CHARTS.

Freed forever from school at 14 for mirroring his beloved Bowie's Ziggy Stardust look, Pete worked at record store and local hangout Probe, vacillating between lavishing praise or berating customers for their musical purchases.

Probe was Burns' entry into Liverpool's music scene. His outrageous look, rake thin with an explosion of Bolan curls, punk D.I.Y. outfits and neo-goth make-up turned heads at every pass. Fronting the local band Nightmares in Wax, he had a minor hit with 'Black Leather' (1980), a raucous mash-up of febrile disco beats and punky guitars.

As Dead or Alive he hit the charts with a sexed-up cover of KC and the Sunshine Band's 'That's The Way I Like It' (1984) before enlisting producers Stock, Aitken and Waterman, then relative unknowns, for the international smash, 'You Spin Me Round (Like a Record)' (1984), a relentless Hi-NRG banger charged with cowbell and topped by Burns' gutsy vibrato.

It was to be Dead or Alive's biggest hit, and their anvil. Despite several other canny pop gems, the band went on diminishing returns. Burns became well known for other reasons, his acid tongue and quick-as-a-whip humour, and, as the 90s progressed, an addiction to tattoos and cosmetic surgery, taking his appearance from androgynous to extreme, like an ancient Egyptian hieroglyph brought to life.

His last decade saw him veer (further) towards tabloid notoriety. Forever threatening a comeback, he was robbed of a last chance with a cardiac arrest in October 2016. Married to best friend Lynn for over 20 years, Burns was absolutely queer in life and outlook, challenging, confounding and confronting the norm. 'My very existence seems to offend and upset imbeciles,' he laughed. 'Which thrills me.'

PETE BURNS

IT'S EASY TO FORGET JUST HOW MUCH CULTURAL FRISSON ANNIE LENNOX (B. 25 DEC. 1954) CREATED WITH HER BAND EURYTHMICS. IN A DECADE LOW ON FEMALE STADIUM FILLERS, LENNOX STOOD TALL AMONGST HER MALE PEERS, WRITING PRISTINE POP HITS PEERLESS IN INTELLIGENCE, CHANGING HER IMAGE TO SUPPORT EACH RELEASE.

Lennox had left Scotland's Aberdeen for a place at London's Royal Academy of music, where, as a budding flautist, she excelled, but lacked direction or inspiration. A chance encounter with guitarist Dave Stewart led to Lennox fronting the Tourists, who scored a minor hit with a pedestrian cover of the Dusty Springfield's single 'I Only Wanna Be With You' (1979).

Eurythmics was a more sophisticated creature, taking a holistic approach to their creative output. With MTV creating global stars through music video, Lennox and Stewart were perfectly in control of their imagery, Lennox transforming from the corporate androgyny of 'Sweet Dreams (Are Made of This)' (1983), the barefooted ingénue of 'Here Comes The Rain Again' (1984) to the stubbled hustler AND cabaret girl of 'Who's that Girl' (1983), the edge-of-nervous breakdown housewife/Texan-girl dreamer of 'Beethoven (I Love To Listen To)' (1987).

Unfairly lumped in as a 'gender bender' of the 80s pop movement, Lennox's play with imagery was far more conversational. With each progressive release Eurythmics expanded their creative range, expanding beyond their synth-fuelled origins, touching on soul, rock, gospel and dance.

Lennox's distinctive voice, expressive, bell-clear and soulful was matched by her band's formidable live reputation and her provocative stage presence, embraced by both gay and straight audiences alike.

Post Eurythmics Lennox continues to enjoy fertile success as solo chanteuse, as well as using her fame to champion LGBTQ+ rights, charitable campaigns and to raise funds and awareness for HIV/AIDS causes, particularly for women and children in Africa.

ANNIE LENNOX

★★ QUEER ICON ★★

HEAVY METAL'S AGGRESSIVE SOUND AND ITS CARTOON-LIKE POSTURING CAN LEAD TO BROAD GENERALISATIONS ABOUT THE BANDS AND THEIR FANS. THE GENRE LONG STOOD TRIAL AS WHIPPING BOY FOR THE CONSERVATIVE RIGHT, ACCUSED OF EVERYTHING FROM UNDERMINING FAMILY VALUES TO ENCOURAGING SUICIDE IN CHILDREN.

It might come as a surprise to non-metal followers that Rob Halford (b. 25 Aug. 1951), powerful belter of Judas Priest and self-described 'stately homo of heavy metal' belongs to our fold.

It was a surprise to the metal world too, when in 1998, Halford finally allowed himself to speak openly about his sexuality, letting it slip in an interview with MTV. Trepidatious of the response to his split moment decision, Halford was overcome and uplifted with the positive response from the metal community and his sizeable fanbase.

The relief was palpable. Years 'in the shadows' had caused him great anguish. Despite Judas Priest's massive success (they were at peak-Priest during the 80s) Halford felt incredibly isolated and depressed, seeking refuge in booze and drug abuse right up until hitting rehab after an overdose on painkillers in 1986.

Ironically, Halford's sexual repression informed Judas Priest's reputation as revolutionaries in heavy metal fashion. In 1978, he began to don a look that was part leather-and-studs rocker, part S&M kink that would become heavy metal de rigueur for the decade ahead.

Things reached peak, and incidentally camp excess, when in 1990 Halford entered the stage in Toronto on a Harley Davidson in leather and shades, ran into the drum riser, and broke his nose. He soldiered on regardless, but bowed out with the band for a good 10 years, attending to solo work and side projects.

In the cultural landscape of queer musicians, those gadding about in Heavy Metal are relatively light on the ground. Halford's coming out was the first to challenge long-held beliefs about heavy metal musicians and its fans.

ROB HALFORD

THE WHIRL AND FLOURISH OF RUFUS WAINWRIGHT (B. 22 JULY 1973) DELIGHTS AND CONFOUNDS IN EQUAL MEASURE. WITH EIGHT ACCLAIMED STUDIO ALBUMS, EXTENSIVE TOURS AND SOUNDTRACK WORK, HIS BAROQUE, FILIGREED POP FLIRTS ALONG THE EDGES OF MAINSTREAM SUCCESS.

Born into Canadian folk-music royalty, unsurprisingly Wainwright showed musical talent from an early age, tinkling the ivories aged six. By his early teens he was performing with The McGarrigle Sisters and Family, a folk group featuring Wainwright, his mother, aunt and sister Martha.

Working Montreal's club circuit for a stint, Wainwright's demos eventually found their way into the hands of a major label. Wainwright toiled away for two years on his debut, boiling down over 50 songs to make up his 12-track eponymous album, released in 1998.

Rufus was the newest, shiniest, gayest musician of the moment. Decamping to New York, his 2001's *Poses* was written during an extended stay at the Chelsea Hotel. Romantic wishes, greed for sex, his quest for fame and his burgeoning addiction to crystal meth all informed the album's writing. Not unlike his seedy accommodation, Wainwright was coming apart at the seams. Unresolved trauma from a sexual assault in London as teenager had lead to sexual abstinence, and then excess in every aspect of his life, his meth use even leading to him temporarily losing his sight.

Coming back down to earth saw three albums in four years, *Want One* (2003), *Want Two* (2004), featuring the shocking and entertaining 'Gay Messiah', possibly Wainwright's apex queer moment. *Release The Stars* (2007) his biggest pop moment yet. In 2006 Wainwright inhabited the songs of Judy Garland, performing her entire 1961 Carnegie Hall show, note-for-note, exposing her music and queer legacy to a new generation. The resulting live album, *Rufus Does Judy at Carnegie Hall* (2007), earned him a Grammy nomination.

In the decade since, Wainwright has married, become a father and written an opera, *Prima Donna*, which made its debut in 2009.

RUFUS WAINWRIGHT

WHEN INDIGO GIRLS SING TOGETHER THEIR VOICES LINK LIKE PINKIES, THE SOUND OF FRIENDS WHO'VE PERFORMED TOGETHER FOR MOST OF A LIFETIME. FOR MORE THAN 30 YEARS AMY RAY (B. 12 APRIL 1964) AND EMILY SALIERS (B. 22 JULY 1963) HAVE DELIVERED THEIR MASTERFUL FOLKY ROCK, BOTH ON RECORD AND STAGE TO A DEVOTED FANBASE.

Having met in junior school in Decatur, Georgia, by high school they were singing together, busting their chops at talent shows and performing underage at local bars under the less zingy monikers of 'Saliers & Ray' and 'The B-Sides'. They plumped for Indigo Girls during their university days at Atlanta, squeezing in acoustic gigs at local hangouts between studies.

After a decade of synth-driven pop, the cult of the singer-songwriter was back in fashion. The likes of Michelle Shocked, Suzanne Vega and 10,000 Maniacs' Natalie Merchant were all enjoying a sustained minute, grazing the charts and all over college radio. The yin yang of Indigo Girls' songwriting (they wrote songs separately, not together) gave them some real chiaroscuro, with Salier's abstracted introspection a foil to Ray's more up-front rock 'n' roll approach.

By their second album, the eponymous *Indigo Girls* (1989) they were signed up to a major label. The album broke double platinum in six months of release and got two Grammy nods. They won Best Contemporary Folk but lost out on Best New Artist to those jammy miming bastards in cycling shorts, Milli Vanilli.

So began a long cycle of awards, success, and seemingly endless touring, all the while presenting as two blue jeans girls from Georgia, eschewing music industry glitz in favour of authenticity, on and off stage.

As two out and proud lesbians, Indigo Girls long ago accepted the mantle of social responsibility as part of their DNA. They have long championed LGBTQ+ rights, those of Native Americans (co-founding the Honor The Earth campaign) and the environment, and hosted scores of fundraising concerts.

INDIGO GIRLS

From the studded trenchcoat, bandana and bikini briefs combo of *Dirty Mind* (1980) to his nude-amongst-the-flowers of *Lovesexy* (1988), Prince challenged notions of what made a man sexy. His furry chest and sharp beard were often matched with a face full of make-up and big hoop earrings. He liked his underpants on the (very) small side, and flirted with high heels (he was mini, to be fair), stockings, lace and purple EVERYTHING, the colour of princes and kings.

Prince chipped away at masculine and feminine, playing with both identities and showing how interchangeable they were. 'If I Was Your Girlfriend' (1987) saw his vocals pitch-shifted up to androgyny, imaging a more intimate relationship as his female lover's platonic girlfriend.

At one point of his career, as part of a protracted spat with his record label Prince even went as far as changing his name to an unpronounceable Love Symbol, unifying male and female 'sex' symbols, defying categorisation even by language.

His proficiency as a musician and output as a recording artist was unparalleled. For the 40 albums he released exploring different sounds, textures, and genres, there were as many side projects and experiments that didn't see the light of day. The way Prince actively straddled so many different sexual and gender identities across these many albums, and their respective videos, artwork and live performances, displayed his need to be recognised as an ongoing work in progress.

While less liberal in his later years, Prince's exploration in androgyny was an inspiration for many members of the LGBTQ+ community, setting off their own journeys through music, gender and sexual identity.

PRINCE

★★ QUEER ICON ★★

'STANDING IN THE WAY OF CONTROL' (2006) REMAINS GOSSIP'S BEST KNOWN CALLING CARD, ITS FUNKY WALKING BASS AND CHOPPY GUITAR LAYING THE WAY FOR BETH DITTO (MARY BETH PATTERSON; B. 19 FEB. 1981) TO RIP LOOSE WITH AN UNBRIDLED, SOULFUL VOCAL.

The track was Ditto's angry response to the Federal Marriage Amendment where Republican politicians were attempting to outlaw same-sex marriage in the US: an indie-dance call to arms and a crossover pop hit.

Ditto's upbringing in Arkansas was a cut and paste shuffle between volatile relatives and a backdrop of baby popping, bible bashing and poverty. She felt forever the outsider: ostracised for her weight, her burgeoning beliefs and her confused sexuality.

Though high school remained hellish she survived through a gang of punky queer misfits, who wore their outsider status with pride and introduced Ditto to the indie counterculture world of D.I.Y. fanzines and mixtapes. In 1999 Ditto left for Olympia, Washington, a beacon for gay-positive counterculture. With fellow Arkansas escapees guitarist Nathan Howdeshell, and drummer Kathy Mendoça, they formed Gossip.

A choir nerd at school, Ditto had tried to dull her voice down to a wisp. With Gossip, she embraced it for all its soulful, gutsy glory. Her stage presence was a lightning bolt to the staid indie scene of the late Noughties.

With 'Standing in the Way of Control' (2006) Ditto went big time – embraced by the public, fashion houses, and the LGBTQ+ community. Ditto quickly became a press favourite. Her appearance, proudly nude, on the cover of indie-rag *NME*, lipstick kiss on bum, was one of the last iconic covers for the magazine. Ditto had her own make-up range, fashion line and even advice column.

While her solo debut is yet to match Gossip's 'Standing in the Way of Control' or 'Heavy Cross' (2009), Ditto continues to tear up pop's rule book to make it big on her own terms.

BETH DITTO

IF LINDA PERRY (B. 15 APRIL 1965) HAD A DOLLAR FOR ANYONE WHO'S ASKED HER 'WHAT'S GOING ON?' SHE'D BE, WELL, EVEN RICHER THAN SHE ALREADY IS.

With the mega-success of 4 Non Blondes's debut single 'What's Up?' (1992) she was delivered a poisoned chalice, a song laser etched on people's psyches, impossible to escape anywhere in the world, and even more difficult to replicate in success.

Seattle's Grunge scene had tendrilled its influence over America. MTV had reached new heights in the 'alternative' realm, breaking 'out there' artists and launching into reality TV with 'The Real World' (1992). Alternative culture was mainstream, and 4 Non Blondes were the perfect alternative guinea pigs, strange steampunky hats and all, unwittingly thrown onto its bonfire.

After a couple of years promoting less memorable singles from *Bigger, Better, Faster, More!* (1992) the band returned to the studio at attempt a follow up. In 1995, 4 Non Blondes inevitably combusted. Perry forged a solo path, releasing *In Flight* (1996) and *After Hours* (1999), neither gaining significant success or acclaim. For lazy male label executives, Perry was too hard to market away from the Non Blonde gang, an out lesbian of unpigeonholable heritage, heavily inked, uninterested in toning herself down for a straight audience.

Happily, Perry had a second life. Re-born as writer and producer to the stars, she created a string of hits, almost exclusively for 'outside the box' female artists. She penned and produced the Grammy-nominated 'Beautiful' (2002) for Christina Aguilera, its theme of personal empowerment resonating deeply with both straight and LGBTQ+ fans. P!nk's 'Get The Party Started' (2001), well, got the party started, and the geniusly throwaway of Gwen Stefani's 'What You Waiting For?' (2004) was like Lene Lovich fronting Missing Persons. She also wrote 'One Word' (2005) for Kelly Osbourne, but we won't hold that against her.

Outside of being one of the industry's most respected writer and producers her Linda lends support organisations such as the LA Gay and Lesbian Center and also the Art of Elysium, a foundation using artistic creativity as the catalyst for change.

LINDA PERRY

WITH BIKINI-CLAD BOYS AND GIRLS WHO SURFED BOARDS, FROM THEIR FIRST SINGLE, 'ROCK LOBSTER', THE B-52S (SELF-PROCLAIMED 'WORLD'S GREATEST PARTY BAND'), WERE INHERENTLY QUEER WITH EVERYTHING THEY TOUCHED.

A creative democracy formed over a shared cocktail in a Chinese restaurant in 1976, The B-52s (vocalists Fred Schneider, Kate Pierson and Cindy Wilson), Ricky Wilson (guitars) and Keith Strickland (drums), were a make-your-own-fun outfit from the staid confines of Athens, Georgia.

Packing half a dozen songs and an unschooled approach to their instruments, the band's first gig (a house party on Valentine's Day) was met with wild acclaim: their keyboard stabs, weirdly tuned guitar, and call and response vocals were lighting bolt of New Wave attitude.

Their songs were nonlinear, sometimes atonal and completely irresistible. Their first two albums *The B-52s* (1979) and *Wild Planet* (1980) were well received – post-punk, girl group harmonies and surfer twang combined like a campy transmission beamed from another planet. Their outre styling – dayglo colours, wigs and man-made fibres (they couldn't afford to dress any other way) played a huge part in the thrift-store chic boom.

As the 80s progressed, the band was relegated to the fringes of mainstream. The loss of beloved guitarist Ricky Wilson to AIDS in 1985, his illness not revealed until upon his death, was devastating (Cindy was Ricky's sister) and saw the band retreat into a creative hiatus.

A decade on from their debut The B-52s returned triumphantly as bona fide mainstream stars, the slightly slicker *Cosmic Thing* (1989) album offering spawning three monster singles 'Love Shack', 'Roam' and the wistful melancholy of 'Deadbeat Club'. The split and soar of their harmonies and the shimmy of their wild tiki rhythms spoke to legions of fans, from big cities to tiny towns as disconnected as their own.

A directive to follow your bliss, 'We were saying it was OK to be different by just living it', explains Strickland, 'Being gay was just a part of it... Just do your thing and your sexual orientation is just a part of it.'

THE B-52S

FOR TEENS IN 60S BRITAIN, MUSIC, FASHION AND ART WERE PORTALS INTO SELF-EXPRESSION, VEHICLES OF A MORE INDIVIDUALISTIC AND PERMISSIVE SOCIETY. UNTIL 1967, MALE HOMOSEXUAL ACTIVITY WAS STILL PUNISHABLE BY PRISON. FOR YOUNG TOM ROBINSON (THOMAS GILES ROBINSON; B. 1 JUNE 1950), A 'GOOD' BOY FROM A MIDDLE CLASS CAMBRIDGE FAMILY, HIS SEXUAL AWAKENING FILLED HIM WITH SUCH SHAME AND DREAD IT LEAD TO A NERVOUS BREAKDOWN.

Music became Robinson's therapy. Witnessing the anarchic energy of an early Sex Pistols gig, he dumped his acoustic group Café Society and formed the politically charged Tom Robinson Band (TRB), aligning themselves with Rock Against Racism, Amnesty International, and advocacy for LGBTQ+ equality.

Enjoying a Top 5 hit with the single '2-4-6-8 Motorway' (1977) (extolling the joys of the long distance lorry driver), they followed with the live EP *Rising Free* (1978) featuring 'Glad to Be Gay'.

It was the world's first gay protest song, and it was marvellous. Its four verses flashed angrily through discrimination at the hands of the police force, the hypocrisy of the British media, the ongoing violence against LGBTQ+ individuals and a call for solidarity over complacency, fear and internalised shame.

The perennially uptight BBC banned 'Glad to Be Gay' on the radio (John Peel, an inspiration to Robinson in his darkest hours as a teen, broke ranks and played it). On Capital Radio it was 'most requested' on the listener-voted Hit line chart for six weeks.

In the years since Robinson has forged a successful as a broadcaster. Now identifying as bisexual, married to a woman and with two children, 40 years later he still is a vehement champion of LGBTQ+ rights, most recently rallying a crowd to Downing Street to welcome new Prime Minister and homophobe-on-record Theresa May with, of course, a searing rendition of 'Glad to Be Gay'.

TOM ROBINSON

WITH THE SMITHS, STEVEN PATRICK MORRISSEY (B. 22 MAY 1959) ROSE OUT OF MANCHESTER TO RULE THE HEARTS AND MINDS OF YOUTH THE WORLD OVER. FROM THE CHIME OF JOHNNY MARR'S GUITAR TO MORRISSEY'S KEENING LYRICS AND DISTINCT VOCALS, THE COMET TAIL OF THE BAND'S SOUND STILL CARRIES OVER TO THIS DAY.

A late bloomer, raised on a steadfast diet of literature, social dissolution and pop music, Morrissey took his own awkwardness and put it under the microscope for the world to see.

His sharp wit, matched with the depth of his sincerity, invited listeners to leave the real world and lose themselves to self-depreciating humour, thwarted desires and ambitions. A world where a drive home could be loaded with cataclysmic feeling, where leaving a nightclub alone was truly the end of days. Things were at once wonderful and terrible and his fans felt them keenly.

Bequiffed and lanky, sporting woman's blouses, thick-rimmed NHS specs, his jeans' back pocket spilling over with long sprigs of gladioli and occasionally, a chunky-as-hell hearing aid, Morrissey rejected the conventional tropes of rock 'n' roll sexiness. The band's record sleeves often ran with a thread of homoeroticism, from underground icons from Warhol's Factory, to matinee idols and Narcissus like male beauties.

Morrissey was a staunch vegetarian, and vehemently anti-Thatcher and anti-monarchy. Though a self-professed celibate, Morrissey's brand of nerd was sexy to his fans. Live performances would see him lose his shirt or have it ripped from him by overly ardent fans, who leapt onto stage in a desperate attempt for a flashpoint moment of connection with their idol.

After four peerless studio albums, The Smiths disbanded and Morrissey continued on what has been, for the most part, a successful solo career. Sadly, the lyrical themes for which he was first and most loved, sincerity and depth of feeling, have drifted into an acrimonious muddle, filled with contradiction and mistrust of the world around him.

MORRISSEY

★★ QUEER ICON ★★

Chapman grew up in Cleveland, Ohio, raised by her mother and older sister. Showing a love for music from an early age, her mother bought her a ukulele (later pinched by a neighbouring kid down the road).

When Chapman was school age, Cleveland was introducing racial intergration into its school system, and tensions were fraught. Finding refuge by throwing herself into her studies, Chapman was awarded 'A Better Chance', a scholarship to move away to the prestigious Wooster School in Connecticut, after which she earned a full scholarship to Tufts University.

At college, she started to write and perform her own music, and at 22 she signed a record deal. First single 'Fast Car' (1988) drew from her insights from life on both sides of the poverty line. Its depiction of the struggle out of deprivation was a modern protest song: folk-pop by a black feminist performer.

Armed only with her acoustic guitar, Chapman took the song to Nelson Mandela's 70th Birthday Tribute, bringing London's Wembley Stadium and millions of TV viewers worldwide to a silenced hush. 'Fast Car' leapt into the top 10 in both the US and UK and her eponymous debut album (1988) with its other hits of 'Talkin' Bout a Revolution' and 'Baby Can I Hold You' would sell over 10 million copies, making Chapman a global star.

While winning another Grammy in 1997 for the romantically themed 'Give Me One Reason' (1995), it's the personally politically charged first album for which she is best remembered. 'Fast Car' has become a standard, from dancehall version (Foxy Brown), devastating spare incantation (Xiu Xiu), to acoustic crowd pleasers by Justin Bieber and Sam Smith.

While her private life remains guarded, throughout her career Chapman has been outspoken advocate for gender, racial and LGBTQ+ equality.

TRACY CHAPMAN

IN THE 70S, FOR THE GAY COMMUNITY, THE CAREFREE ABANDON OF THE DANCE FLOOR PROVIDED REFUGE FROM THE DAILY DISENFRANCHISEMENT WITHIN STRAIGHT SOCIETY.

On the crest of the disco wave rode Village People. Stamping out a team of clones like gay superheroes, Village People's image became one of the most recognisable in popular culture. For unsuspecting straight fans, the cowboy, Indian, construction worker, cop, leatherman and soldier were more familiar as part of a toy figurines than West Village fantasties.

Entrepreneur Jacques Morali and business partner Henri Belolo witnessed the explosion of macho imagery in New York's Greenwich Village. They enlisted the young (straight) Victor Willis as session vocalist for an album, *Village People* (1997), aimed squarely for the gay market. The appeal of songs like 'San Francisco (You've Got Me)' (1977) crossed over to a straight audience, and prompted American Bandstand to request a TV performance. Cue Morali mustering a group of macho men who could sing, dance and (in the ads they'd placed) 'have a mustache'.

Onto a good thing, their label Casablanca Records pumped out no less than four Village People albums between 1978 and 1979. 'Macho Man' (1978) was a huge hit and its call to arms follow up 'Y.M.C.A.', one of the decade's biggest songs. In a truly bonkers turn of events, the US Navy let the band take over the San Diego Navy base, its crew guest-starring in the band's video for 'In The Navy' (1979). The navy had considered the song for their recruitment advertising – wincingly hilarious as the U.S. gay military ban wasn't lifted until 1993.

Lead 'person' Willis departed as plans were afoot for a feature film *Can't Stop the Music* (1980), which fizzed spectacularly at the box office. To say that the band's attempts at a comeback were received with a lukewarm response would be generous. Despite Village People's genesis and imagery, whether they were a gay group is still up for conjecture, even among their members. Irrespective, the band's success is indebted to the support given to them through disco's LGBTQ+ community.

VILLAGE PEOPLE

Cabaret performances with her ensemble Antony and The Johnsons bore the fruit of her original songs, garnering support from Current 93's David Tibet (who released *Antony and The Johnsons* (2001)) and alternative music godfather Lou Reed, with whom she toured as a vocalist.

Anohni took full flight with her second album, 2005's Mercury Prize winning *I am a Bird Now*. The cover, featuring Warhol muse Candy Darling on her deathbed, surrounded by flowers, was the perfect foil to its music, a sweeping exploration of sorrow, friendship and transformation. Boy George, Rufus Wainwright and Lou Reed himself contributed, cementing Anohni to a lineage of legendary artists from New York's downtown scene.

Anohni's exquisite chamber pop went from circling largely around the personal to becoming universally conscious in approach and thinking. 'Blind', her strident guest vocal collaboration with Hercules and Love Affair, singularly put that band on the map, and was Pitchfork's Best Track of 2008.

In 2016 she began publicly using her 'spirit name', the mononymous Anohni, and identifying as a transgender woman. The album accompanying her comeback, the extraordinary *Hopelessness* (2016), was a seismic shift in sound and subject. Yielding to synth pads and brittle beats, Anohni swathed them candy-sweet melodies and then, Hydra-like, rained hellfire on toxic masculinity, and societal, technological and ecological malaise.

Her outspoken brilliance has not been confined to music. With Future Feminists, she's gathered collective of performers and artists, whose output challenges straight, masculine societal hierarchies: 'I truly believe that unless we move to feminine systems of governance, we don't have a chance on this planet'.

ANOHNI

'LIFE ISN'T ABOUT FINDING YOURSELF, IT'S ABOUT CREATING YOURSELF.' TROYE SIVAN (B. TROYE SIVAN MELLET; 5 JUNE 1995) IS AN INTERNET BOY WONDER, A WIDE-EYED, TOUSLE-HAIRED, STRING BEAN POST-GENRE POP SINGER AND WRITER WHO'S FORGED A CREDIBLE CAREER VERY MUCH ON HIS OWN UNORTHODOX TERMS.

Relocating to Australia from South Africa as a toddler, Sivan was home-schooled and given free reign to pursue singing and performing. Acting bubbled up first, including the lead in the South African 'Spud' trilogy, where as a late-blooming teen of the title, he navigated the many challenges and joys of high school life.

Social media and Sivan went hand in hand, with YouTube his main vehicle for creative expression. After a solid five years of posts, he switched gears from singing and general silliness to confessional, his candid coming out vlog of 2013 further cementing the exchange of trust between Sivan and his already millions of devoted followers.

Social media also represented a new way to launch his musical career. Sivan's ability and willingness to present his art informed by his personal growth is a winning formula. Bringing in collaborators and vocalists, pulling in subtle flourishes of EDM and other genres cast his musical net wider again. Sivan's lyrics and his music's downtempo, electronic tinges hold a mirror up to the experiences of his fans, like diary entries on the joy and pain of encroaching adulthood.

His first release through a major label, 'TRXYE' (2014), was an instant hit worldwide. The *Wild* EP followed in 2015, with his album *Neighbourhood* closing out the year, its single, the yearning 'Youth' is a quest to finding love whatever the cost.

'I'm just trying to show people that you can be queer, live your life, and be happy'.

TROYE SIVAN

BORN IN GEORGIA DURING THE GREAT DEPRESSION, SCRAWNY WITH A PRONOUNCED LIMP AND EFFEMINATE, LITTLE RICHARD (RICHARD WAYNE PENNIMAN; B. 5 DEC. 1932) HAD HIS CARDS STACKED AGAINST HIM. YET HALF A CENTURY LATER, HE'S GONE ON NOT ONLY ENJOY A WILDLY SUCCESSFUL (IF ERRATIC) CAREER IN MUSIC AND ACTING, BUT A MOUNTAIN OF AWARDS AND ACCOLADES, RECOGNISED FOR SHAPING POPULAR MUSIC AS WE KNOW IT.

One of 12 siblings, Richard's family's poverty was buoyed by an unwavering belief in the Lord Almighty. Their fervour for gospel music sunk its hooks into him and in church he found his voice, hooting and hollering with a high pitched scream that belied his diminutive stature. He'd felt feminine from an early age, donning his mother's make-up and clothes, getting thrown out of the house as a teen by his deacon father.

He kicked off his career on the the Chitlin' Circuit, hitting venues in the South that were safe for black performers to visit during the segregation era. His early recordings of live favourites 'Tutti Frutti' (1957) and 'Long Tall Sally' (1957) brought him great mainstream success and attention on both sides of the Atlantic, merging the fervour of gospel with a distinctly secular rhythm and blues sound – the very things rock 'n' roll would go on to be made of.

Richard's subsequent US tours were the first to bring black and white audiences together. Anchored by his piano, he was as camp as he was commanding, whipping audiences into a dancing frenzy, female fans flinging their knickers at him, unperturbed by his confoundingly outré sensibilities – a peacock parade of blouses, capes and jewels, slimline moustaches and make-up.

Though married to women several times over, Richard was open about his relationships with men. 'We are all both male and female. Sex to me is like a smörgåsbord. Whatever I feel like, I go for.' To this day, Little Richard continues to be a mass of contradictions, in and out of love with his Lord, with music and his sexuality.

LITTLE RICHARD

MORE QUEER MUSIC ICONS WHO CHANGED THE WORLD

Bedsit eroticist and torch song troubadour
MARC ALMOND

Stilt-legged avant electro producer and performer
ARCA

Hi-NRG synth and songwriting pioneer
PATRICK COWLEY

Rocking Aussie rambler
COURTNEY BARNETT

The sublimely lovelorn baroque pop of
PERFUME GENIUS

Genre pushing queer rapper/producer
Le1f

Power pop super twins and LGBTQ+ activists
TEGAN & SARA

Raspy voiced rocker
MELISSA ETHERIDGE

Teen-angst popster turned hit writer
LESLEY GORE

Blue-eyed soul sensation
DUSTY SPRINGFIELD

Legendary caberet chanteuse
JOSEPHINE BAKER

The revelatory house reinvention of
HERCULES AND LOVE AFFAIR

Avant garde, anti-establishment industrialist
GENESIS P-ORRIDGE

Glitzy singalong piano showman
PETER ALLEN

Legendary caberet chanteuse
ST VINCENT

Mesmerising dance soothsayer
and cellist
ARTHUR RUSSELL

The electronic post disco
church of
LARRY LEVAN

The experiments of
electronic pranksters
MATMOS

THANKS

Grateful thanks and love to Kentaro, Dan, and Geoffrey for all your advice and encouragement. Thanks to the wonderful (and patient) Hardie Grant team: Kate, Kajal, Eila and Molly. Thank you to Michele for the illustrations, and to Claire for the art direction.

ABOUT THE AUTHOR

Will Larnach-Jones has worked in the music industry for 20 years, touring the world with bands of every genre. He's worn many hats throughout that time – manager, publicist, agent, A&R, music programmer, marketing 'guru' and (rubbish) DJ.